SENT
with
LOVE
SPECIAL DELIVERY

Letters to:

From:

Date begun:

Letters to My
SON

♥

WITH LOVE FROM:

....

PETER PAUPER PRESS, INC.
WHITE PLAINS, NEW YORK

PETER PAUPER PRESS

In 1928, at the age of twenty-two, Peter Beilenson began print-ing books on a small press in the basement of his parents' home in Larchmont, New York. Peter—and later, his wife, Edna—sought to create fine books that sold at "prices even a pauper could afford."

Today, still family owned and operated, Peter Pauper Press continues to honor our founders' legacy—and customers' expectations—of beauty, quality, and value.

Designed by Heather Zschock

Copyright © 2019
Peter Pauper Press, Inc.
202 Mamaroneck Avenue
White Plains, NY 10601 USA
All rights reserved
ISBN 978-1-4413-2901-1
Printed in China

7 6 5 4 3 2 1

Visit us at www.peterpauper.com

Dear Parent,

So many thoughts and emotions revolve around our experiences with our children, from bits of wisdom to feelings of love or concern. Here's the place to record all of these, as well as hopes and memories.

Begin when they're newborn, or pick up when they're teenagers. Use this as your private journal, or create a keepsake to share.

XOXO

Dear

Love,

Dear

Love,

Dear

Love,

Dear

Love,

Date:

Just a note:

XOXO

Date:

Just a note:

XOXO

Just a note:

XOXO

Just a note:

XOXO

Date:

Dear

Love,

Dear

Love,

Date:

Dear

Love,

Dear

Love,

Dear

Love,

Dear

Love,

Dear

Love,

Dear

Love,

Dear

Love,

Date:

Just a note:

XOXO

Date:

Just a note:

XOXO

Date:

Just a note:

XOXO

Date:

Just a note:

XOXO

Dear

Love,

Dear

Love,

Dear

Love,

Dear

Love,

Dear

Love,

Dear

Love,

Dear

Love,

Dear

Love,

Date:

Dear

Love,

Just a note:

XOXO

Just a note:

XOXO

Date:

Just a note:

XOXO

Date:

Just a note:

XOXO

Dear

Love,

Dear

Love,

Dear

Love,

Dear

Love,

Dear

Love,

Dear

Love,

Dear

Love,

Dear

Love,

Dear

Love,

Date:

Just a note:

XOXO

Date:

Just a note:

XOXO

Date:

Just a note:

XOXO

Date:

Just a note:

XOXO

Dear

Love,

Dear

Love,

Dear

Love,

Dear

Love,

Dear

Love,

Dear

Love,

Dear

Love,

Date:

Dear

Love,

Dear

Love,

Date:

Just a note:

XOXO

Date:

Just a note:

XOXO

Date:

Just a note:

XOXO

Date:

Just a note:

XOXO

Dear

Love,

Dear

Love,

Dear

Love,

Dear

Love,

Dear

Love,

Dear

Love,

Dear

Love,

Dear

Love,

Dear

Love,

Date:

Just a note:

XOXO

Date:

Just a note:

XOXO

Date:

Just a note:

XOXO

Date:

Just a note:

XOXO

Dear

Love,

Dear

Love,

Dear

Love,

Dear

Love,

Dear

Love,

Dear

Love,

Dear

Love,

Dear

Love,

Date:

Dear

Love,

Date:

Just a note:

XOXO

Date:

Just a note:

XOXO

Just a note:

XOXO

Just a note:

XOXO

Dear

Love,

Date:

Dear

Love,

Dear

Love,

Dear

Love,

Dear

Love,

Dear

Love,

Dear

Love,

Dear

Love,

Dear

Love,

Just a note:

XOXO

Just a note:

XOXO

Date:

Just a note:

XOXO

Date:

Just a note:

XOXO

Dear

Love,

Dear

Love,

Dear

Love,

Date:

Dear

Love,

Dear

Love,

Dear

Love,

Dear

Love,

Date:

Dear

Love,

Dear

Love,

Date:

Just a note:

XOXO

Date:

Just a note:

XOXO

Date:

Just a note:

XOXO

Date:

Just a note:

XOXO

Dear

Love,

Dear

Love,

Date:

Dear

Love,

Date:

Dear

Love,

Dear

Love,

Dear

Love,